Eucharistic Prayers
For Children

Eucharistic Prayers For Children

With 20 Suggested Liturgies

Rev. William J. Freburger
and
James E. Haas

Ave Maria Press
Notre Dame, Indiana 46556

ABOUT THIS BOOK

The purpose of this book is to make the Eucharistic Prayers for Children the richest resource possible for the worshiping community of young people. The themes of the individual celebrations (Part Two) were chosen because they are the themes woven throughout the Eucharistic Prayers. These relationships will be an obvious advantage in catechesis. The "Introduction" to the Eucharistic Prayers urges that the texts themselves be used as a tool for instruction. Each of the prayers differs in format and content. For a particular celebration, the most appropriate rule for choosing is to select the prayer that best illustrates the theme or uses language or images allied to it.

The three new Eucharistic Prayers for Children are another sign of the importance which the Church sees in promoting the growth of a liturgical spirit in its younger members. We can surely expect further signs of a similar nature in the future, because worship for children is an accepted priority. These new Eucharistic Prayers will help make worship an even more rewarding experience for all—both children and adults—who call Jesus Lord and wait in joyful hope for his coming.

ACKNOWLEDGMENTS:

Much work goes into the creation of a book such as this, and we would like to thank the following persons, without whose contributions *Eucharistic Prayers for Children* could not have been written: Bonnie Carman, Amy Goudy, Lynne Haas and Sr. Janaan Manternach.

English translation of *Eucharistic Prayers for Masses With Children,* copyright © 1975, International Committee on English in the Liturgy, Inc. All rights reserved.

Nihil Obstat: Rev. Gordon E. Truitt
        Censor Deputatus

Imprimatur: Most Rev. William D. Borders, D.D.
        Archbishop of Baltimore

L.C.C.C.N. 75-39414
I.S.B.N. 0-87793-109-7

Contents

Part One: Eucharistic Prayers for Children

Part Two: Suggested Celebrations for Children

Appendix:

Part One

Eucharistic Prayers
for
Children

Commentary on the
New Eucharistic Prayers for Children
by William J. Freburger

The Eucharistic Prayer is "the center and highpoint of the entire celebration," "a prayer of thanksgiving and sanctification" in which "the whole congregation joins Christ in acknowledging the works of God and in offering the sacrifice." That succinct definition from the *General Instruction of the Roman Missal* (no. 54) condenses an understanding of our worship which is continued in the three new Eucharistic Prayers for Children.

For over a thousand years the Latin rite of the Catholic Church employed only one Eucharistic Prayer, the Roman Canon, the "norm" of celebration for both adults and children. During that millennium celebrants said the Latin text, by rubric, in the hushed tones that many adults recall today with nostalgia as contributing to the "mysterious" atmosphere of the Catholic Mass. The liturgical principles of Vatican II's *Constitution on the Sacred Liturgy* effected two major reforms in this tradition: the proclamation of the Latin text of the Canon in a public speaking voice, and its eventual translation into the vernacular. These steps highlighted the merits of this venerable prayer, but also exposed its structural weaknesses.

The introduction of three additional Eucharistic Prayers in 1968 greatly enriched the Latin rite. These new compositions, ancient in inspiration, allowed scope for elements neglected in the Roman Canon or minimally treated in its various prefaces, for instance, more direct expression of thanksgiving, acknowledgment of the role of the Spirit, explicit mention of the eschatological dimension of the Eucharist. However, it soon became apparent that none of these four formulas (the Roman Canon—now Eucharistic Prayer I—and the three new prayers of 1968) was suitable for celebrations with children. These Eucharistic Prayers were composed for adults. This is the liturgy into which children are initiated, but the actual texts do not allow for adaptation to the mentality and circumstances of young congregations.

The Roman Congregation for Divine Worship acknowledged this situation in its *Directory for Masses with Children* (November 1, 1973) and promised the creation of Eucharistic Prayers designed exclusively for celebrations with children. That promise is fulfilled in the three new Eucharistic Prayers which are the subject of this discussion. These prayers were first published on November 1, 1974, together with two Eucharistic Prayers for Masses with the theme of reconciliation. The Holy See approved the English translation for use in the United States on June 5, 1975.

An "Introduction" accompanies the text of the prayers and explains their purpose: "The text of Eucharistic Prayers adapted for children should help them to participate with greater benefit in the Masses celebrated for adults" (no. 1). Since growth into the spirit of prayer within the adult Eucharistic assembly is the goal of this liturgical initiation, it is not enough merely to *use* these Eucharistic Prayers in celebrations with children. Care must be taken to foster that "full, active and conscious participation" for which the Second Vatican Council called.

Both catechists and celebrants should be familiar with the principles contained in the *Directory for Masses with Children*. Guided by these, a concerned and knowledgeable celebrant will exercise his presidency to promote the active participation of the children. Adaptations of gestures and bodily posture, as well as the increased number of acclamations in the new Eucharistic Prayers, can assist in this regard, transforming mere listeners into active worshipers.

All efforts should conspire to introduce children into the *style* of liturgical prayer. Because the Eucharist is ritual, it involves repetition. Because it is bodily, it involves signs. Because it is the action of Christ, it is sacramental. Because it is also the action of the people of God, it is ecclesial. It glorifies God and sanctifies persons. Catechesis must endeavor to communicate an understanding and an appropriation of all these elements.

The following paragraphs describe briefly the history of the Eucharistic Prayer and the nature of its various parts. Each of the three new prayers is then presented in summary fashion.

On the night before he died, Jesus ate with his disciples. In the course of this meal, he took bread and blessed it, broke it, called it his body, and gave it to his disciples to eat. After the meal, he took a cup filled with wine and gave thanks, called it his blood, and gave it to the disciples to drink. Then he told them, "Do this in memory of me."

This simple description is rich with echoes that have persisted to our day. Thanksgiving, blessing, meal, body and blood in sacrifice, breaking of bread, memorial—tradition has handed them on to us. In one sense, Jesus himself was doing nothing out of the ordinary, for he used the pattern of prayer familiar to Jews both in public worship and in daily life. That pattern was the "blessing" (*berakah* in Hebrew), a form of prayer in which God was "blessed" for what he had done for his people. This remembrance of God's favors carried strong overtones of praise and thanksgiving. That gratitude for past deeds spilled over into hope for the future; the blessing engaged God's faithfulness by asking him to manifest his power.

Whether at public worship, in elaborate prayer (such as the *Magnificat* and the *Benedictus* in Luke 1: 46-55 and 69-79) or in the simple blessings of everyday life, the pattern was the same: an exclamation of praise, a memorial of the past, a petition for the future, and a concluding summary of praise. As Jesus moved from village to village, announcing the good news of the kingdom and manifesting its presence in his healings, he had many opportunities to pray according to that pattern. The custom of the people made each daily meal into a festival, for it transformed a human biological necessity into an act of worship by means of the blessing: "Blessed are you, Lord, God of heaven and earth, for this bread which we eat." Many were the times that Jesus took bread, blessed it, broke it, and gave it to his hosts and disciples.

But, on that Thursday night before he died, Jesus said something he had never said before. He told his disciples, "Do this in memory of me." That command transformed this "last supper" into the first of many suppers. It made an extraordinary meal, the Jewish Passover, an even more extraordinary celebration, the Christian Eucharist. That command initiated a tradition of 19 centuries which still lives in our midst. Today, we can claim what Paul first wrote to his community at Corinth:

> I received from the Lord what I handed on to you, namely, that the Lord Jesus on the night in which he was betrayed took bread, and after he had given thanks, broke it and said, "This is my body, which is for you. Do this in remembrance of me." In the same way, after the supper, he took the cup, saying, "This cup is the new covenant in my blood. Do this, whenever you drink it, in remembrance of me." Every time, then, that you eat this bread and drink this cup, you proclaim the death of the Lord until he comes!

Our celebration of the Eucharist is the supper of Holy Thursday, not just because we say what Jesus said, but because we do the same thing he did: We bless God by praising and thanking him and we look to him for salvation, trusting in the promises he has made. The words and actions of Jesus are recalled and accomplished in the celebration because Jesus is the promised salvation.

This basic pattern is the content of the tradition that has been handed on to us; but, as it was being passed from generation to generation, the tradition became the "traditions." Natural laws of development and codification allowed various groups to enshrine their spiritual experiences and cultural emphases within their rites. The Roman Canon, elaborated in its substance by the seventh century, is only one example of the pattern as it became incarnated down through history. Other traditions within the Church manifest varying approaches and differing features in their prayers. But in all communities that celebrate the Eucharist, the central prayers are similar in essentials.

In the decade since the Second Vatican Council, the Latin rite of the Catholic Church has experienced an intensification of Eucharistic creativity. The order for the celebration of the Eucharist was enriched with three additional Eucharistic Prayers in 1968 and entirely revised in 1969 according to the principles of the *Constitution on the Sacred Liturgy.* That revision was accompanied by an explanatory document, the *General Instruction,* which outlined the theology of the celebration of the Eucharist and presented the pastoral rationale for the revision.

According to paragraph no. 55 of the *General Instruction of the Roman Missal,* the chief elements of the Eucharistic Prayer are these:

"a) Thanksgiving (expressed especially in the preface): In the name of the entire people of God, the priest praises the Father and gives him thanks for the work of salvation or for some special aspect of it in keeping with the day, feast, or season.

"b) Acclamation: United with the angels, the congregation sings or recites the *Sanctus.* This acclamation forms part of the Eucharistic Prayer, and all the people join with the priest in singing or reciting it.

"c) Epiclesis: In special invocations the Church calls on God's power and asks that the gifts offered by men may be consecrated, that is, become the body and blood of Christ and that the victim may be a source of salvation for those who are to share in communion.

"d) Narrative of the institution and consecration: In the words and actions of Christ, the sacrifice he instituted at the Last Supper is celebrated, when under the appearances of bread and wine he offered his body and blood, gave them to his Apostles to eat and drink, and commanded them to carry on this mystery.

"e) Anamnesis: In fulfillment of the command received from Christ through the Apostles, the Church keeps his memorial by recalling especially his passion, resurrection, and ascension.

"f) Offering: In this memorial, the Church—and in particular the Church here and now assembled—offers the victim to the Father in the Holy Spirit. The Church's intention is that the faithful not only offer the spotless victim but also learn to offer themselves and daily to be drawn into ever more perfect union, through Christ the Mediator, with the Father and with each other, so that at last God may be all in all.

"g) Intercessions: The intercessions make it clear that the Eucharist is celebrated in communion with the whole Church of heaven and earth, and that the offering is made for the Church and all its members, living and dead, who are called to share in the salvation and redemption acquired by the body and blood of Christ.

"h) Final doxology: The praise of God is expressed in the doxology which is confirmed and concluded by the acclamation of the people."

This is the structure of the Christian *berakah,* the "blessing" of God that we call the Eucharistic Prayer. The new prayers for use in Masses with children are the result of this articulation of our traditions. What are these prayers like? How are they to be celebrated? What points do they supply for catechesis? It should be noted that these texts are not a radical departure from our Eucharistic experience. They are *Eucharistic Prayers* for *children;* they are not miniaturized versions of the adult prayers. Composed for celebrations with children, they attempt to honor both the purpose of the occasion and the special requirements of the congregation.

The three Eucharistic Prayers for Children have a group of characteristics in common. The Latin text published by the Holy See was never intended for liturgical use; its purpose was to serve as a guide for translators around the world, determining for them the substance and general form of the prayers. Since the Latin language does not possess a special style for speaking with children, this original text could only hope to indicate the basic simplicity of structure and style. In translation, the spirit of each language would determine the specific adaptations to be made.

In all three prayers, the words of Jesus recited over the bread and wine are the same as in the adult Eucharistic Prayers. However, before the command "Do this in memory of me," a phrase has been inserted: "then he said to them." Immediately after the genuflection, the celebrant continues with the anamnesis, at the end of which comes the (memorial) acclamation. The purpose of this rearrangement is to enable the children to distinguish more clearly what is said over the bread and wine and what refers to the continuation of the celebration. In addition, this postponement of the acclamation makes obvious the connection between the Lord's command and the memorial (anamnesis) pronounced by the priest.

The most striking feature of the prayers is the increased number of acclamations. An acclamation is an outburst of assent or affirmation. It is usually joyful, and the nature of it demands singing. The prayers themselves do not offer any music for these statements of assent. Therefore, it is imperative that existent music be freely used and simple musical settings be quickly developed so that the acclamations can be employed to full advantage. In most cases, the texts provide a cue line leading into the acclamation, e.g., in Prayer II: "With Jesus we sing your praise." The celebrant will have to emphasize these phrases, either by tone of voice or by singing. It should be noted that the prayers do not consistently indicate a lead-in to the acclamations. Prayer II, for instance, contains some acclamations that are not introduced by a cue line.

The "Introduction" to the texts describes each of the prayers in general terms, pointing out what seems to be the main feature. Prayer I is characterized by a great simplicity. It strives to promote familiarity with the *Sanctus* acclamation by dividing it into parts and by using the individual strophes to break up the body of its lengthy preface. Prayer II affords more opportunity for participation by including an increased number of acclamations. Prayer III allows for seasonal and occasional inserts at three points in the text. The present text offers a set of inserts for the Easter season, and invites conferences of bishops to compose similar sets for other times and seasons.

Both Prayer II and Prayer III do not have a memorial acclamation as such. In its place, these prayers use an acclamation of praise ("We praise you, we bless you, we thank you" or "Glory to God in the highest") whose purpose is to highlight the nature of the Eucharistic Prayer as one of praise and thanksgiving. The celebrant may further emphasize these characteristics by adding special reasons for giving thanks, tailored to the occasion, before the initial dialogue of the preface. This practice has already been encouraged by the *Directory for Masses with Children* (no. 22).

An examination of the texts of the new Eucharistic Prayers for Children shows how the elements of a Eucharistic Prayer, listed in no. 55 of the *General Instruction of the Roman Missal,* are arranged in these compositions. It also makes apparent what is candidly acknowledged in the "Introduction" to the prayers: These prayers contain "all the elements of a Eucharistic Prayer . . . *with some very infrequent exceptions"* (no. 4, italics added).

Prayer I begins with a preface of 50 lines, broken in three places by acclamations based on the *Sanctus* of adult Eucharistic Prayers. The purpose of this arrangement, as the "Introduction" explains, is "to accustom children more easily to the *Sanctus"* (no. 23). After the opening dialogue, the body of the preface begins with a statement of purpose—to give thanks and praise —and presents a number of motives for that: beauty and happiness, daylight, earth and its peoples, and life itself which is God's gift. With daylight is paired a reference to God's "word which lights up our minds." The mention of revelation sits strangely in the midst of this listing of natural gifts. This first part of the preface ends with a summary, that God loves us, which forms a natural cue for the first strophe of the *Sanctus* acclamation.

The preface continues by citing Jesus as gift of the Father, supreme proof that God does love us and does not forget us. The Son is described in concrete images inspired by the gospel: He cured the sick, cared for the poor, wept with the sad, forgave sinners, and loved everyone. A final image engages the assembly present, "He took children in his arms and blessed them," leading into an acclamation which embodies the second strophe of the *Sanctus*, "Blessed is he who comes in the name of the Lord."

The third section of the preface represents an exception to the usual structure of our Eucharistic Prayers; for, to the union of our praise with the heavenly liturgy is coupled a mention of unity with the whole Church, with the Pope, and with the local bishop. Unity with the Church is more usually cited as part of the intercessions in our adult Eucharistic Prayers. Because of its explicit use here in the preface, its later citation in this prayer is an attenuated one: "Remember Christians everywhere." A familiar cue line, "Now we join with (the saints) and with the angels to adore you as we sing," closes the preface and introduces the full *Sanctus* acclamation.

After a brief transition paragraph, the epiclesis invokes the Spirit upon the gifts. The institution narratives are the same as in the adult Eucharistic Prayers, with the exception mentioned earlier: the insertion of "then he said to them" before the command and the postponement of the memorial acclamation. The celebrant continues with the anamnesis, the memorial of the paschal mystery and the offering of "the bread that gives us life and the cup that saves us." It is only at this point that the celebrant issues the invitation, "Let us proclaim our faith." With this arrangement, the memorial acclamation stands out more strongly as a proclamation of faith in the paschal mystery, rather than merely in the mystery of the bread and wine transformed into the body and blood of Christ.

The second part of the epiclesis is a very simple prayer for the "fruits of communion." The intercessions follow, but their point is blunted somewhat since communion with the whole Church has been shifted to the preface. Among the intercessions is a remembrance for "everyone who is suffering from pain or sorrow." As the *Directory for Masses with Children* had already indicated (no. 39), the text of the doxology is taken from the adult Eucharistic Prayers.

This first Eucharistic Prayer for Children is a very short and simple text, outstanding for its use of concrete images. Its acclamatory emphasis is on the *Sanctus*. Unfortunately, because that acclamation is interwoven with a lengthy preface, the prayer may seem "top-heavy": of the hundred lines of text, close to half are devoted to the preface and its acclamations.

Prayer II is constructed for more participation through acclamations. There are 12 acclamations in the course of the prayer, an average of one for every seven lines of presidential text. The preface is divided into four sections, each marked by an acclamation. The arrangement is similar to Prayer I, but the preface text is much shorter here. The first three sections present motives for thanks and praise (you love us, you give us this world, you sent us Jesus). The phrase "With Jesus we sing your praise" signals the acclamation. Two possibilities are suggested: "Glory to God in the highest" or "Hosanna in the highest." The fourth section of the preface is a summary:

> For such great love
> we thank you with the angels and saints
> as they praise you and sing.

The full text of the *Sanctus* acclamation follows.

The prayer continues with an interesting "embolism," an extended consideration of the last strophe of the *Sanctus*. "Blessed is he who comes in the name of the Lord." The emphasis is on Jesus, "Blessed be Jesus whom you sent," but the remembrance of his works is not stated so concretely as in Prayer I. Here the terms are more abstract and "theological." The "embolism" concludes with a mention of the Spirit and his work in our midst. The acclamation inserted at this point is an inclusion device, "Blessed is he who comes in the name of the Lord." Unfortunately, it is not preceded by a cue line.

A brief invocation of the Spirit, "to change these gifts of bread and wine into the body and blood of Jesus," leads naturally into the institution narratives. The prayer introduces an Eastern flavor into this section. As the priest shows the consecrated host to the assembly, the children sing, "Jesus has given his life for us." The pattern is repeated as the chalice is shown. The "Introduction" directs that these "acclamations which are inserted after the words of the Lord recited over the bread and wine must be considered and sung as a common meditation on the Eucharistic mystery" (no. 24). In place of a memorial acclamation, Prayer II offers an acclamation of praise, "We praise you, we bless you, we thank you," which is repeated four times (with no lead-in!): after the anamnesis, after the second part of the epiclesis, after the intercessions, and after the prayer for eschatological fulfillment. The intercessions contain a remembrance for "all those we do not love as we should." Immediately after the fourth repetition of the acclamation of praise, the celebrant sings the doxology.

Prayer II obviously lives up to its description and purpose, to provide more opportunities for participation through acclamations. Fully 25 percent of the text is acclamatory material. A unique feature adapted from the Eastern rites is the acclamation inserted after the words over the bread and over the wine. The prayer has a very distinct "Jesus emphasis," underlined by the extended "blessing" of Jesus that comes between the preface and the first invocation of the Spirit.

Prayer III has a close, structural resemblance to the adult texts with which we are already familiar. It has the option of seasonal inserts that may be substituted at three points (preface, transition between preface and institution narratives, intercessions). The text itself supplies a set of these inserts for Eastertime. Oddly enough, the preface of this prayer is not very soteriological in the motives it cites for thanks and praise: God has given us each other, thus making friendship and sharing possible. The insert that replaces these motives in Eastertime is much stronger, for it focuses on the resurrection of Jesus and the pledge of eternal life that is given to us. After the *Sanctus* acclamation, the prayer continues with a "thanks" for Jesus whose work is identified in gnoseological terms: he "opened our eyes and our hearts to understand that we are brothers and sisters and that you are father of us all." An unfortunate defect in this prayer is the lack of a true epiclesis; the Father is asked to make the gifts holy, but the Spirit is not invoked. Like the second Eucharistic Prayer for Children, Prayer III does not have a memorial acclamation. The celebrant's anamnesis occurs in three parts: The first part mentions the death and resurrection (twice!); the second refers to the present state of Jesus (living in glory and present in the Church); the third refers to his coming again in glory. Each of these sections is to be greeted with the suggested acclamation, "Glory to God in the highest." Both the prayer for the "fruits of communion" and the intercessions are very brief. Once again, the doxology follows the text of the adult Eucharistic Prayers.

Prayer III seems to be the weakest of the three, both theologically and liturgically. Yet, the possibility of creating seasonal and occasional inserts offers the opportunity to correct these weaknesses. The omission of the Spirit in the consecratory epiclesis is to be deplored. The extended anamnesis with its acclamations can be a source of variety at this point and the foundation for instruction in the meaning of the paschal mystery and its "memorial."

These Eucharistic Prayers for Masses with children have been approved *ad experimentum* for a period of three years, until the end of 1977. For this reason, the texts will not appear in the various editions of the *Sacramentary* (altar missal); instead, the Bishops' Committee on the Liturgy has published them in a separate fascicle. The actual use of these prayers in celebration will reveal various weaknesses of structure and infelicities of expression. Such findings ought not to go to waste. Experiences, suggestions and emendations should be forwarded to the Bishops' Committee on Liturgy (1312 Massachusetts Avenue, N.W., Washington, D.C. 20005) to assist in future editing of these Eucharistic Prayers and the creation of other compositions adapted for those children whose brothers and sisters Jesus took in his arms and blessed.

Text of
Eucharistic Prayers
for
Masses With Children*

INTRODUCTION

1. The text of eucharistic prayers for children should help them to participate with greater benefit in the Masses celebrated for adults.

Thus the Directory for Masses with Children decreed that some texts of the Mass are never to be adapted for children "lest the difference between Masses with children and Masses with adults become too great." Among these texts are the "acclamations and responses of the people to the greetings of the priest."[1] The dialogue of the preface of these eucharistic prayers is therefore always the same as in Masses for adults and the same holds for the *Sanctus,* apart from what is stated in nos. 18 and 23 below.

2. In accordance with the apostolic constitution, *Missale Romanum,* the words of the Lord in each formula of the canon are likewise the same.[2]

3. Before the words, "Do this in memory of me," a sentence has been introduced: "Then he said to them." This is to enable children to distinguish more clearly what is said over the bread and wine and what refers to the continuation of the celebration.

4. Each of the three eucharistic prayers for Masses with children contains all the elements of a eucharistic prayer in accordance with no. 55 of the General Instruction of the Roman Missal, with some very infrequent exceptions.

5. Not only are all the required elements present but also those elements which are always expressed in accordance with tradition, for example, in the memorial or invocation of the Spirit, but in a simpler style of language adapted to the understanding of children.

6. Although a simpler style of language was adopted, the authors always had in mind the importance of avoiding the dangers of childish language which would jeopardize the dignity of the eucharistic celebration, especially in the case of words to be said by the celebrant himself.

7. Because the principles of active participation are in some respects

even more significant for children, the number of acclamations in the eucharistic prayers for Masses with children has been increased in order to enlarge this kind of participation and make it more effective.[3] This has been done without obscuring the nature of the eucharistic prayer as a *presidential* prayer.

8. Because it is very difficult for only one eucharistic prayer to be used effectively throughout the world in Masses with children, in view of the cultural differences and the character of various peoples, it seemed appropriate to propose three texts with different features (explained in nos. 23-25 below).

Translations of These Prayers into Various Languages

9. It is for the episcopal conference to choose one of the drafts proposed here and to see that the text is translated into the vernacular so that it will correspond fully to pastoral, pedagogical, and liturgical needs. Such a translated text may not be introduced into liturgical use before it has been confirmed by the Apostolic See.

10. It is desirable that this work of translation be given to a group of men and women who are competent not only in liturgical matters but also in the pedagogical, catechetical, literary, and musical aspects of this task.

11. The committee of translators should always remember that the Latin text in this case is not intended for liturgical use. Therefore it is not simply to be translated.

The Latin text determines the purpose, substance, and general form of these prayers, and these should be the same in the translations into the various languages. Features proper to the Latin language (which never developed a special style of speaking with children) are never to be carried over into the vernacular texts intended for liturgical use, specifically, the Latin preference for the so-called hypotactic construction, the rather ornate and repetitious style, and the so-called *cursus*. All aspects of the style of speech should be adapted to the spirit of the respective language as well as to the manner in which one speaks with children concerning matters of great importance. These principles are all the more pertinent in the case of languages which are far removed from Latin, especially non-Western languages. An example of translation for each eucharistic prayer is given in a Western language as a possible aid to the translator.

12. In translating these texts careful distinction should be made between the several literary genre which occur in the eucharistic prayer, namely, the preface, intercessions, acclamations, etc., in accordance with the principles which were expressed in the instruction of January 25, 1969, for the translation of liturgical texts.[4]

13. In addition, episcopal conferences should see that the new *musical settings* are prepared for the parts of the prayers to be sung by the children, in accordance with the culture of the region.

Liturgical Use of These Prayers

14. The use of these prayers is strictly limited to Masses celebrated with children. The right of the bishop, which is determined in the Directory for Masses with Children,[5] remains, however, intact.

15. The eucharistic prayer which seems best suited to the needs of the children in each nation should be chosen from among the three texts: either the first for its greater simplicity, the second for its greater participation, or the third for the variations it affords.

16. New acclamations may be easily introduced into liturgical use if, with a cantor or one of the children leading, they are repeated with everyone singing or reciting them. Care should be taken in the preparation of texts in the vernacular, however, that acclamations are provided with a simple introduction, for example, a common phrase to invite the acclamation.

17. In place of the new acclamations which are found in these eucharistic prayers the episcopal conferences may introduce others provided they have the same spirit.

18. It is necessary that children should also learn to sing or recite the *Sanctus,* but the rule remains in effect that sometimes it is permissible to use for this song "musical settings to appropriate translations approved by the competent authority, even if they are not in complete agreement with the liturgical text, in order to facilitate the participation of the children."[6] In various regions where there is the practice of chanting the *Sanctus* in a responsorial manner, the episcopal conferences may permit this.

19. The position of the acclamation of the faithful which is made at the end of the consecration has been somewhat changed. This is done for pedagogical reasons. So that the children may clearly understand the connection between the words of the Lord, "Do this in memory of me," and the memorial pronounced by the priest, the acclamation, whether a memorial acclamation or one of praise, is not made until after the memorial (*anamnesis*) has been spoken.

20. To encourage participation by the children, it is permissible, in accordance with the Directory for Masses with Children, to insert special reasons for thanksgiving before the dialogue of the preface.[7] The regulations of no. 33 of the Directory also apply for participation through gestures and bodily postures. Above all great stress should be placed upon internal participation, and what is said in no. 23 of festive, fraternal, meditative celebration is especially true of the eucharistic prayer.

21.   To encourage this internal participation which should be a deep concern of the pastors of children, it is necessary that the celebration be preceded and followed by careful catechetical instruction. Among the texts which will clearly express this catechesis to children, a prominent place belongs to the eucharistic prayers which will be used as the high point in the celebrations.[8]

22.   The rubrics for the individual eucharistic prayers are given in the Latin text only. All of them are to be inserted in the vernacular text.

Special rubrics for concelebration, as are found in the four eucharistic prayers already introduced, are lacking in these prayers. In view of the psychology of children it seems better to refrain from concelebration when Mass is celebrated with children.

A)   Eucharistic Prayer I

23.   In order to accustom children more easily to the *Sanctus,* the first eucharistic prayer divides it into the parts which are concluded by the acclamation, "Hosanna in the highest." In accordance with no. 16 above, these acclamations may be sung or recited with a cantor or one of the children leading. The third time the entire song may be sung or recited by all. After the memorial of this prayer, in place of the simpler acclamation given in the text, one of the acclamations approved for the four eucharistic prayers may be sung.

B)   Eucharistic Prayer II

24.   In the second eucharistic prayer while the *Sanctus* and the memorial acclamation are retained, other optional acclamations may be used. Acclamations which are inserted after the words of the Lord recited over the bread and wine must be considered and sung as a common meditation on the eucharistic mystery.

C)   Eucharistic Prayer III

25.   In the third eucharistic prayer variable parts for only one occasion are indicated, namely, for the Easter season. It is intended, however, that similar variable parts be approved by the episcopal conferences for other seasons and occasions and put into use after the requisite confirmation by the Apostolic See in accordance with no. 10 of the circular letter on eucharistic prayers.[9] In preparing these texts care should be taken that the three parts (preface, part after the *Sanctus,* invocation of the Spirit) have an appropriate internal unity.

After the consecration the same acclamation occurs three times in the same way so that the character of praise and thanksgiving of the entire prayer may be suggested to the children.

NOTES

1. See Directory for Masses with Children, No. 39: *AAS* 66 (1974) 41-42.
2. *AAS* 61 (1969) 219.
3. See Directory for Masses with Children, No. 22: *AAS* 66 (1974) 36.
4. See Consilium for the Implementation of the Constitution on the Liturgy, *Instruction on Translation of Liturgical Texts*, January 25, 1969: *Notitiae* 5 (1969) 3-12.
5. See Directory for Masses with Children, No. 19: *AAS* 66 (1974) 35.
6. See *ibid.*, No. 31: *AAS* 66 (1974) 39.
7. See *ibid.*, No. 22: *AAS* 66 (1974) 37.
8. See *ibid.*, No. 12: *AAS* 66 (1974) 33.
9. *AAS* 65 (1973) 344.

Eucharistic Prayer for Children

I

The priest begins the eucharistic prayer. With hands extended he sings or says:

The Lord be with you.

People: And also with you.

Priest: Lift up your hearts.

People: We lift them up to the Lord.

Priest: Let us give thanks to the Lord our God.

People: It is right to give him thanks and praise.

The priest, with hands extended, continues:

God our Father,
you have brought us here together
so that we can give you thanks and praise
for all the wonderful things you have done.

We thank you for all that is beautiful in the world
and for the happiness you have given us.
We praise you for daylight
and for your word which lights up our minds.
We praise you for the earth,
and all the people who live on it,
and for our life which comes from you.

We know that you are good.
You love us and do great things for us.
[So we all sing (say) together:

Holy, holy, holy Lord, God of power and might,
heaven and earth are full of your glory.
Hosanna in the highest.]

The priest, with hands extended, says:

Father,
you are always thinking about your people;
you never forget us.
You sent us your Son Jesus,
who gave his life for us
and who came to save us.
He cured sick people;
he cared for those who were poor
and wept with those who were sad.
He forgave sinners
and taught us to forgive each other.
He loved everyone
and showed us how to be kind.
He took children in his arms and blessed them.
[So we are glad to sing (say):

Blessed is he who comes in the name of the Lord.
Hosanna in the highest.]

The priest, with hands extended, continues:

God our Father,
all over the world your people praise you.
So now we pray with the whole Church:
with N., our pope and N., our bishop.
In heaven the blessed Virgin Mary,
the apostles and all the saints
always sing your praise.
Now we join with them and with the angels
to adore you as we sing (say):

All say:

Holy, holy, holy Lord, God of power and might,
heaven and earth are full of your glory.
Hosanna in the highest.
Blessed is he who comes in the name of the Lord.
Hosanna in the highest.

The priest, with hands extended, says:

God our Father,
you are most holy
and we want to show you that we are grateful.

We bring you bread and wine

He joins his hands and, holding them outstretched over the offerings, says:

and ask you to send your Holy Spirit to make these gifts

He joins his hands and, making the sign of the cross once over both bread and chalice, says:

the body + and blood of Jesus your Son.

With hands joined, he continues:

Then we can offer to you
what you have given to us.

On the night before he died,
Jesus was having supper with his apostles.

He takes the bread and, raising it a little above the altar, continues:

He took bread from the table.
He gave you thanks and praise.
Then he broke the bread, gave it to his friends, and said:

He bows slightly.

Take this, all of you, and eat it:
this is my body which will be given up for you.

He shows the consecrated host to the people, places it on the paten, and genuflects in adoration. Then he continues:

When supper was ended,

He takes the chalice and, raising it a little above the altar, continues:

Jesus took the cup that was filled with wine.
He thanked you, gave it to his friends, and said:

He bows slightly.

> Take this, all of you, and drink from it:
> this is the cup of my blood,
> the blood of the new and everlasting covenant.
> It will be shed for you and for all men
> so that sins may be forgiven.
> Then he said to them:
> Do this in memory of me.

He shows the chalice to the people, places it on the corporal, and genuflects in adoration. Then, with hands extended, the priest says:

> We do now what Jesus told us to do.
> We remember his death and his resurrection
> and we offer you, Father, the bread that gives us life,
> and the cup that saves us.
> Jesus brings us to you;
> welcome us as you welcome him.
>
> Let us proclaim our faith:

All say:

> Christ has died,
> Christ is risen,
> Christ will come again.

Then, with hands extended, the priest continues:

> Father,
> because you love us,
> you invite us to come to your table.
> Fill us with the joy of the Holy Spirit
> as we receive the body and blood of your Son.
>
> Lord,
> you never forget any of your children.
> We ask you to take care of those we love,
> especially of N. and N.,
> and we pray for those who have died.
>
> Remember everyone who is suffering from pain or
> sorrow.
> Remember Christians everywhere
> and all other people in the world.
>
> We are filled with wonder and praise

when we see what you do for us
through Jesus your Son,
and so we sing:

He joins his hands, takes the chalice and the paten with the host and, lifting them up, he sings or says:

Through him,
with him,
in him,
in the unity of the Holy Spirit,
all glory and honor is yours,
almighty Father,
for ever and ever.

The people respond:

Amen.

Eucharistic Prayer for Children

II

The priest begins the eucharistic prayer. With hands extended he sings or says:

> The Lord be with you.

People: And also with you.

Priest: Lift up your hearts.

People: We lift them up to the Lord.

Priest: Let us give thanks to the Lord our God.

People: It is right to give him thanks and praise.

The priest, with hands extended, continues:

> God, our loving Father,
> we are glad to give you thanks and praise
> because you love us.
> With Jesus we sing your praise:

All say:

> Glory to God in the highest.
> *or:*
> Hosanna in the highest.

The priest says:

> Because you love us,
> you gave us this great and beautiful world.
> With Jesus we sing your praise:

28

All say:

Glory to God in the highest.
    or:
Hosanna in the highest.

The priest says:

Because you love us,
you sent Jesus your Son
to bring us to you
and to gather us around him
as the children of one family.
With Jesus we sing your praise:

All say:

Glory to God in the highest.
    or:
Hosanna in the highest.

The priest says:

For such great love
we thank you with the angels and saints
as they praise you and sing (say):

All say:

Holy, holy, holy Lord, God of power and might,
heaven and earth are full of your glory.
    Hosanna in the highest.
Blessed is he who comes in the name of the Lord.
    Hosanna in the highest.

The priest, with hands extended, says:

Blessed be Jesus, whom you sent
to be the friend of children and of the poor.

He came to show us
how we can love you, Father,
by loving one another.
He came to take away sin,
which keeps us from being friends,
and hate, which makes us all unhappy.

He promised to send the Holy Spirit,
to be with us always
so that we can live as your children.

29

All say:

Blessed is he who comes in the name of the Lord.
Hosanna in the highest.

He joins his hands and, holding them outstretched over the offerings, says:

God our Father,
We now ask you
to send your Holy Spirit
to change these gifts of bread and wine

He joins his hands and, making the sign of the cross once over both bread and chalice, says:

into the body + and blood
of Jesus Christ, our Lord.

The night before he died,
Jesus your Son showed us how much you love us.
When he was at supper with his disciples,

He takes the bread and, raising it a little above the altar, continues:

he took bread,
and gave you thanks and praise.
Then he broke the bread,
gave it to his friends, and said:

He bows slightly.

Take this, all of you, and eat it:
this is my body which will be given up for you.

He shows the consecrated host to the people while all say:

Jesus has given his life for us.

He places the consecrated host on the paten, and genuflects in adoration. Then he continues:

When supper was ended,

He takes the chalice and, raising it a little above the altar, continues:

Jesus took the cup that was filled with wine.
He thanked you, gave it to his friends, and said:

He bows slightly.

Take this, all of you, and drink from it:
this is the cup of my blood,
the blood of the new and everlasting covenant.
It will be shed for you and for all men
so that sins may be forgiven.

He shows the chalice to the people while all say:

Jesus has given his life for us.

The priest continues:

Then he said to them:
Do this in memory of me.

*He places the chalice on the corporal and genuflects in adoration. Then,
with hands extended, the priest says:*

And so, loving Father,
we remember that Jesus died and rose again
to save the world.
He put himself into our hands
to be the sacrifice we offer you.

All say:

We praise you, we bless you, we thank you.

The priest says:

Lord our God,
listen to our prayer.
Send the Holy Spirit
to all of us who share in this meal.
May this Spirit bring us closer together
in the family of the Church,
with N., our pope,
N., our bishop,
all other bishops,
and all who serve your people.

All say:

We praise you, we bless you, we thank you.

The priest says:

> Remember, Father, our families and friends (. . . .),
> and all those we do not love as we should.
> Remember those who have died (. . .).
> Bring them home to you
> to be with you for ever.

All say:

> We praise you, we bless you, we thank you.

The priest says:

> Gather us all together into your kingdom.
> There we shall be happy for ever
> with the Virgin Mary, Mother of God and our mother.
> There all the friends
> of Jesus the Lord
> will sing a song of joy.

All say:

> We praise you, we bless you, we thank you.

He joins his hands, takes the chalice and the paten with the host and, lifting them up, he sings or says:

> Through him,
> with him,
> in him,
> in the unity of the Holy Spirit,
> all glory and honor is yours,
> almighty Father,
> for ever and ever.

The people respond:

> Amen.

Eucharistic Prayer for Children

III

The priest begins the eucharistic prayer. With hands extended he sings or says:

> The Lord be with you.

People: And also with you.

Priest: Lift up your hearts.

People: We lift them up to the Lord.

Priest: Let us give thanks to the Lord our God.

People: It is right to give him thanks and praise.

The priest, with hands extended, continues:

> We thank you,
> God our Father.
>
> *You made us to live for you and for each other.
> We can see and speak to one another,
> and become friends,
> and share our joys and sorrows.
>
> And so, Father, we gladly thank you
> with every one who believes in you;
> with the saints and the angels,
> we rejoice and praise you, saying:

During the Easter season this section may be replaced by number 1 on page 37.

All say:

Holy, holy, holy Lord, God of power and might,
heaven and earth are full of your glory.
Hosanna in the highest.
Blessed is he who comes in the name of the Lord.
Hosanna in the highest.

The priest, with hands extended, says:

Yes, Lord, you are holy;
you are kind to us and to all men.
For this we thank you.
We thank you above all for your Son, Jesus Christ.

*You sent him into this world
because people had turned away from you
and no longer loved each other.
He opened our eyes and our hearts
to understand that we are brothers and sisters
and that you are Father of us all.

He now brings us together to one table
and asks us to do what he did.

He joins his hands and, holding them outstretched over the offerings, says:

Father,
we ask you to bless these gifts of bread and wine
and make them holy.

He joins his hands and, making the sign of the cross once over both bread and chalice, says:

Change them for us into the body + and blood of
Jesus Christ, your Son.

With hands joined, he continues:

On the night before he died for us,
he had supper for the last time with his disciples.

During the Easter season this section may be replaced by number 2 on page 37.

He takes the bread and, raising it a little above the altar, continues:

> He took bread
> and gave you thanks.
> He broke the bread
> and gave it to his friends, saying:

He bows slightly.

> Take this, all of you, and eat it:
> this is my body which will be given up for you.

He shows the consecrated host to the people, places it on the paten, and genuflects in adoration. He takes the chalice and, raising it a little above the altar, continues:

> In the same way he took a cup of wine.
> He gave you thanks
> and handed the cup to his disciples, saying:

He bows slightly.

> Take this, all of you, and drink from it:
> this is the cup of my blood,
> the blood of the new and everlasting covenant.
> It will be shed for you and for all men
> so that sins may be forgiven.
> Then he said to them:
> Do this in memory of me.

He shows the chalice to the people, places it on the corporal and genuflects in adoration. Then, with hands extended, the priest says:

> God our Father,
> we remember with joy
> all that Jesus did to save us.
> In this holy sacrifice,
> which he gave as a gift to his Church,
> we remember his death and resurrection.

> Father in heaven,
> accept us together with your beloved Son.
> He willingly died for us,
> but you raised him to life again.
> We thank you and say:

All say:

> Glory to God in the highest *(or some other suitable acclamation of praise).*

The priest says:

> Jesus now lives with you in glory,
> but he is also here on earth, among us.
> We thank you and say:

All say:

> Glory to God in the highest *(or some other suitable acclamation of praise).*

The priest says:

> One day he will come in glory
> and in his kingdom
> there will be no more suffering,
> no more tears, no more sadness.
> We thank you and say:

All say:

> Glory to God in the highest *(or some other suitable acclamation of praise).*

The priest says:

> Father in heaven,
> you have called us
> to receive the body and blood of Christ at this table
> and to be filled with the joy of the Holy Spirit.
> Through this sacred meal
> give us strength to please you more and more.
>
> Lord, our God,
> remember N., our pope,
> N., our bishop, and all other bishops.
>
> *Help all who follow Jesus
> to work for peace
> and to bring happiness to others.

During this Easter season this section may be replaced by number 3 on page 37.

Bring us all at last
together with Mary, the Mother of God,
and all the saints,
to live with you
and to be one with Christ in heaven.

He joins his hands, takes the chalice and the paten with the host and, lifting them up, he sings or says:

Through him,
with him,
in him,
in the unity of the Holy Spirit
all glory and honor is yours,
almighty Father,
for ever and ever.

The people respond:

Amen.

DURING THE EASTER SEASON

(1)   You are the living God;
you have called us to share in your life,
and to be happy with you for ever.
You raised up Jesus, your Son,
the first among us to rise from the dead,
and gave him new life.
You have promised to give us new life also,
a life that will never end,
a life with no more anxiety and suffering.

(2)   He brought us the good news
of life to be lived with you for ever in heaven.
He showed us the way to that life,
the way of love.
He himself has gone that way before us.

(3)   Fill all Christians with the gladness of Easter.
Help us to bring this joy
to all who are sorrowful.

Part Two

Suggested Celebrations
for
Children

Introduction to the Celebrations

Even though the American Catholic Church has paid special attention to its children for over a century, today is an extraordinary time for young people. We have come to acknowledge their particular need for initiation into the liturgical life of the adult community. This recognition is shared by the whole Church; indeed, it is officially promoted. The *Directory for Masses with Children* (1973) called for specific adaptations to meet the needs of children at worship. Modes of celebration for young Christians may not necessarily reproduce a more formal liturgical style, but such celebration can increase children's appreciation of rituals and symbols, and refine their liturgical sense. The three new Eucharistic Prayers for Children add to our resources for achieving these goals.

Today, then, we can celebrate with children in a way that matches their stages of development. The suggestions and possibilities outlined in this section are geared generally for young people in grades three through seven. Celebrating with children, teaching them to pray, leading them to growth in union with God—these significant tasks take time. They call for preparation and patience; they demand diligence. They mean work.

This dedication is the first requirement for those who would plan, lead and celebrate the Eucharistic Liturgies outlined here (and in other books). What are the other requirements? What else is necessary to lead children to "worship in spirit and in truth"?

Celebrations with children generally should flow out of the religious education or catechetical experience of their age group or class. In many instances, the children should have a part in the creation and design of the celebration. If these celebrations are to promote liturgical growth, the priest/celebrant, the catechist and the worshiping class or group must have a close working relationship. They must know one another; they must be comfortable together.

In developing the liturgy, the catechist will employ a number of pedagogical techniques to prepare for the celebration. Some of these techniques should be used in the course of the homily. They can serve as "seeds" for the homily, but they will take time. Therefore, the leader of the group must be free to spend more than ten minutes in debriefing the activity, or in delivering or sharing the homily with the worshipers. A commitment to celebrate with children is a commitment *to* the children, a commitment to spend the time *with* them *for* them.

In the celebrations suggested here, two activities (one relatively simple, the other more complex) are offered for the preparatory phase. A celebrant's attitude toward the activity selected by the catechist and/or the children has a profound effect on the quality of the homily experience. Since children learn best when their senses are used to the full in the learning experience, these activities are not just time-fillers! If the celebrant can appreciate their benefit, there will be a successful engagement of the children in the celebration.

The priest/celebrant must have a feel for the type of presiding suited to leading children in worship. He must appreciate liturgy as ritual, a pattern of activity that enshrines values and teaches those values experientially through the act of celebrating. While care should be taken to avoid novelty for the sake of getting or keeping attention, a good pastoral-liturgical sense will guide a priest/celebrant in using a broad range of resources. The goal of any liturgical celebration should be to unite the children *both* among themselves *and* with the Church, to bring them *both* knowledge *and* faith, to propose Jesus *both* as example *and* as intimate.

The celebrations include a paragraph entitled "Homily Hints." Hints they are—not the only ideas or insights possible. The homily should revolve around an experience that is familiar to the celebrant. If necessary, the hints presented here can be used, but personal insights can also be developed.

If it takes time to prepare and celebrate the liturgy, time is also necessary to reflect upon the experience following the actual celebration. The outlines include a suggested prayer experience to complete the homily and a follow-up to the celebration itself; ideas for both of these are usually taken from the homily hints or adapted from the pre-celebration activities. Those who plan the celebration should discuss ways in which the follow-up suggestions can be best implemented.

Music is an integral part of worship. Some songs are suggested for each celebration, but, since the music must be closely integrated for the particular occasion, the planners (catechists, celebrant, worshiping group) must establish the range of music to be used. The appendix of this book contains an extensive listing of available recordings. The Eucharistic Prayers for Children demand the use of sung acclamations. Emphasis on the acclamatory nature of the Roman liturgy can provide welcome relief to the "four-hymn syndrome." The statement of the Bishops' Committee on the Liturgy, *Music in Catholic Worship,* offers a variety of suggestions for the use of music in Eucharistic celebrations.

The appendix presents a bibliography of magazine articles, books and media programs for liturgy with children. The liturgical experiences of the American Church during the past decade has created an enormous quantity of material for children's worship. Familiarity with the published items will provide many suggestions and insights for planning worship experiences with and for children. Since so much assistance is already available in published form, the celebrations in this book should be seen as outlines whose purpose is not to repeat what can be readily garnered elsewhere. The planning process will easily fill in the blanks.

Each celebration lists appropriate filmstrips and children's stories for use in catechesis. Only one of the 20 celebrations actually uses a filmstrip at the time of the homily; the other celebrations can be enriched in similar fashion. The usefulness of a particular filmstrip for a celebration will, obviously, be apparent after a prior viewing. The children's stories may be read and discussed before the celebration, or they can be read during the homily time. Young people love to listen to stories. The books suggested here have been chosen for their relationship to the theme and to the level of the learner. They should be used as often as possible. The appendix contains the addresses of the sources for the filmstrips and stories.

James E. Haas

1
Creation

Resources

Songs

"God Made the Animals," Jack Miffleton, *Even a Worm,* W.L.P.
"The Great Lights," Jack Miffleton, *Even a Worm,* W.L.P.
"God Made Us All," Jack Miffleton, *Come Out!,* F.E.L.

Filmstrips

How God Speaks to Us Today, Family Filmstrips
Mystery of Myself and My World, #1, *Children of the Light* Series,
    Roa Films
The All Powerful One, #1, *Kree Finds the Way,* Roa Films
God Exists, Catechetical Guild

Literature

Fisher, Aileen. *Like Nothing At All.* New York: Thomas Y. Crowell, 1962
Lexau, Joan. *More Beautiful Than Flowers.* Philadelphia: Lippincott,
    1966

Preparation

1. About three or four weeks before the liturgy each child in the group can plant forget-me-nots or other pretty flowers in milk carton containers. Over the weeks, they can take responsibility for the plants.

2. Make a list of ten things that complete this sentence: "..................... reminds me that God created the world, because . . ."

Readings

1. Genesis 2:4-6; 1:26-30. God creates man and woman in his own image.
2. Colossians 3:10, 12-14. Likeness to God shines forth in forgiveness and love.
3. Other: Psalm 8, John 1:1-14

Homily Hints

Discuss with the children the steps they took to bring their flowers to bloom. Focus in on ideas relating to man's responsibility for the ongoing creation of the world. Tie in as many reminders of God's creation from the second suggested activity. Children will list such items as sunsets, flowers, animals and people. Share ideas as to how man can continue to create his world.

Prayer Experience

The celebrant can invite the children to complete the following sentence: "Let us thank the Lord for creating ...." Then the group can respond, "Thank you, Lord."

Gifts

Flowers, lists, bread, wine. As the gifts are brought to the altar the celebrant can continue, "Let us thank the Lord for bread and wine, and other gifts in the offerings." Suggestions: a flower grown by one of the children, a pretty stone, picture of one family.

Follow-up

Take the pretty flowers to a neighborhood nursing home.

2
Community

Resources

Songs

"The Spirit Is A-Movin," Carey Landry, *The Spirit Is A-Movin,* N.A.L.R.
"Receive in Your Heart," Lou Fortunate, William H. Sadlier, Inc.
"Love One Another," Germaine Habjan, *Songs of Salvation,* F.E.L.
"What a Great Thing It Is," Ray Repp, *Allelu,* F.E.L.

Filmstrips

A Family, # 10, *Kree Finds the Way,* Roa Films
Baptism: Sacrament of Resurrection, Thomas Klise
Reborn in Christ and *To Live in Christ,* # 2, *Introduction to the Sacraments,* Don Bosco Filmstrips
Billy Beaver and *The Pumpkin Who Was Not a Squash,* from *Holydays and Holidays,* Twenty-Third Publications
This Sunday Party, Thomas Klise

Literature

Lionni, Leo. *Swimmy.* New York: Pantheon, 1963

Preparation

Divide the children into three groups. Each has a specific task. The first can create a drawing around the theme, "Things a Community Can Do Together." Group two can write a paragraph on the theme "Our class is a community because . . ." The third group has the task of creating a mural on the theme, "The Community of Man Works Together for Good Things to Happen." Use magazine pictures, torn paper, newspaper headlines, etc., to create the mural. All groups can bring their drawings, paragraphs and mural to the place of celebration.

Readings

1. Romans 12:14-18. Care and concern are marks of community.
2. Matthew 5:23-24. God looks for mutual love and respect for each other.
3. Other: John 15:11-17

Homily Hints

Encourage children to explain their drawings, read their paragraphs and talk about the mural. Communities work, play, eat, celebrate, pray and do many other things together. Yes, they even fight once in a while. Communities grow because things are done together, and because there is frequently a unifying ideal, goal or person. Jesus is the person around whom the community of the Church is gathered. He has called us to build community in as many ways as possible, hence the mural.

Prayer Experience

Distribute copies of *Desiderata* and then read along as the celebrant says the words thoughtfully.

Gifts

Bread, wine, examples of drawings and paragraphs, NASA photo of earth.

Follow-up

Encourage the children to read *Desiderata* in their spare time and memorize a favorite or most meaning-filled phrase. Ask them to think about an answer to this statement, "One way I can really live the meaning of the words I've chosen is ...."

3
Election

Resources

Songs

"You Are My People," Germaine Habjan, *Songs of Salvation*, F.E.L.
"Great Things Happen," Carey Landry, *Hi God!*, N.A.L.R.

Filmstrips

The Call of Abraham, # 1, Abraham, Father of Believers, Roa Films
Story of Moses Series, Cathedral Films

Literature

Swift, Hildegarde, and Ward, Lynd. *The Little Red Lighthouse and the Great Gray Bridge.* New York: Harcourt, Brace, Jovanovich, 1942

Preparation

1. Ask the children to finish these two sentences: I liked it very much when I was chosen to .... because . . . On the other hand, I didn't like it too much when I was chosen to .... because...

2. Throughout time many persons seem to have been elected or chosen by God through the actions of others to perform certain tasks, acts of heroism, to achieve great holiness. Ask the children to select one such person, read a book about him or her and be prepared to discuss why that person seemed to have been chosen specially by God.

Readings

1. Ezekiel 36:24-28. God chooses his people and cleanses them.
2. 1 Corinthians 12:12-15. Church is a unity through Baptism.

Homily Hints

Talk about the various responses to the sentences. Determine whether they all did the tasks to which they were called. What happened if they didn't meet all the requirements? God called Israel and they responded and were very happy to be his chosen people. However, sometimes what God chose them for didn't measure up to their expectations and they rebelled in various ways. Election implies responsibility. Refer to the different persons from history about whom the children read. Each had talents and used them to accomplish the necessary tasks but they too had moments of grumbling when they didn't think too much of their having been elected. Ask children to relate the stories.

Prayer Experience

Sit quietly and listen to the song "Follow Me" (Mary Travers, Warner Bros. record #7143). Think of God calling people throughout history right down to calling you today.

Gifts

Bread, wine, representative books, completed sentences, ballot box, symbols of authority such as keys or a judge's gavel.

Follow-up

Pray especially for those in authority, from presidents and popes to mayors and moms. Make mom and dad a genuine appreciation badge reading "Congratulations! You're Elected! You're the Best!"

4

God's Presence

Resources

Songs

"I Will Not Forget You," Carey Landry, N.A.L.R.
"God Has Visited His People," James Haas, *Rainbow Songs,* Morehouse-Barlow
"Wonder-full World," James Thiem, F.E.L.

Filmstrips

Jonah, Pflaum Standard
The Wind and the Fire, #5, *Kree Finds the Way,* Roa Films
My Name Is Jesus Series, Roa Films
The Three Hermits, Unit #4, *Lifelines,* Teleketics

Literature

Lamorisse, Albert. *The Red Balloon.* New York: Doubleday, 1969
DeKort, Kees, illus. *Jesus Is Risen.* Minneapolis: Augsburg, 1969

Preparation

1. Write one paragraph describing God and follow it with another paragraph telling of the person who most reminds you of God and why so.

2. Whenever we read the New Testament we read about Jesus doing things so as to make known his Father's will. Before the celebration suggest to the group that they do the things that Jesus taught us to do, as teaching, giving good advice, comforting, forgiving, etc. Ask them to give serious thought to what they do and to be prepared to share their reflections.

Readings

1. Leviticus 26:9-13. God promises to "walk to and fro among us" (N.E.B.).
2. John 16:23-28. The Father loves us.
3. Other: Psalm 41; Romans 5:1-5; Galatians 2:19-20

Homily Hints

Ask the children to share their description of God and, however anonymously, those persons who most remind them of God. What characteristics and virtues occur most frequently. [Author's note: Younger groups of children will be very anthropomorphic. I suggest a careful reading of Ronald Goldman's *Readiness for Religion* (Seabury Press, 1968).] Which of the activities in suggestion number two above relate to the description offered by the children? Allow boys and girls to relate their experiences and share their insights. How do their actions make God present?

Prayer Experience

Ask children to complete the following sentence. One thing new I learned about God today is .... As each child offers his learning everyone responds, "Praise the Lord!"

Gifts

Bread, wine, plant, family photograph.

Follow-up

Recall some of the actions chosen by group members to live out the commands of Jesus. Choose one and make a contract to do it yourself. The contract can read "I .... promise that I will
(name)
.... to bring God present in this world."
(action)

5

Faithfulness

Resources

Songs

"How Good Is the Lord," Carey Landry, N.A.L.R.
"Come Away," Ray Repp, *Mass for Young Americans*, F.E.L.

Filmstrips

Footprints, #8, *Kree Finds the Way,* Roa Films
Story of Moses Series, Cathedral Films
Charles Caterpillar, from *Holydays and Holidays,* Twenty-Third Publications
Hosea: Prophet of Love, #6, *Kings and Prophets,* Roa Films

Literature

Taylor, Theodore. *The Cay.* New York: Doubleday, 1969.

Preparation

1. Before the celebration have each child write the word "faithful" on a piece of paper and then his or her own definition.

2. Recall a story from TV or a book you've read about someone who was faithful to another person, an ideal, a dream, a promise or whatever. What did the person do in the story and how would you respond to this statement, "One thing I learned about faithfulness from the person in this movie, TV show, or book is ...."

Readings

1. Acts 10:38-39. Jesus went about doing good.
2. Matthew 9:18-35. A description of Jesus, dedicated to healing.
3. Other: Hebrews 12:1-3

Homily Hints

What definitions were written by the children and what were some of the learnings gleaned from TV shows, movies and books? Tell a few short stories from the bible or history or the world of literature about people who held fast to their beliefs.

Prayer Experience

After your having listened to them and their having listened to you, suggest that they reflect on their own life experience. In the quiet of their hearts ask them to recall a time they were faithful to an idea, a person, a promise. What did it cost them? Suggest they recall a time when they perhaps didn't keep a promise or failed to deliver even though they could have. What did they lose?

Gifts

Bread, wine, "faithful" definitions.

Follow-up

Select a particular job around the house, school, or neighborhood. Plan to do it for a particular length of time. Be faithful to your contract and think about why you're doing what you've chosen.

6
Light

Resources

Songs

"Then It Dawns on Me," Joe Wise, *Watch With Me,* N.A.L.R.
"Growing," James Haas, *Rainbow Songs,* Morehouse-Barlow
"Even a Worm," Jack Miffleton, *Even a Worm,* W.L.P.
"Bushel Round," Jack Miffleton, *Even a Worm,* W.L.P.

Filmstrips

Introduction to the Sacraments, Don Bosco Filmstrips
The Parables, Twenty-Third Publications
Baptism: Sacrament of Resurrection, Thomas Klise

Literature

Lionni, Leo. *Alexander and the Wind-up Mouse.* Pantheon, 1969

Preparation

1. Let each child do a finger-painting project on the theme, *"God Brings Light to Our Life,"* and ask them to be prepared to talk about their creations.

2. Suggest that each child prepare a collage on the theme, *"Light."*

Readings

1. Isaiah 9:1-7. God gives the light of salvation.
2. John 12:44-47. Jesus is the light.
3. Other: 2 Corinthians 4:1-6.

Homily Hints

The children can explain their finger paintings and collages while the leader asks questions such as: Why is light important? What would life be like without light? Why did Jesus refer to himself as the "light of the world"? We can shed light when people ask us questions, we can be a light to others when we guide them, or we can be the light at the end of a tunnel, as when people need us a great deal after a particularly difficult situation in their lives.

Prayer Experience

The Lord sheds light on the lives of us all. Gather the group around a Christ-candle and sing or recite the acclamation, "You are life, Lord our God, tell us of your kingdom of love."

Gifts

Bread and wine, candle, flashlight, picture of the sun.

Follow-up

Spend a few moments before sleep to think about your day. Did you bring light to someone's life or did you darken it? Were you thoughtful or thoughtless? Be happy with the good you've done and give serious thought to improving the areas in your life that you know to be in need of attention.

7

Sacrifice

Resources

Songs

"God Is Love," Clarence Rivers, *People's Mass Book,* W.L.P.
"Love One Another," Germaine Habjan, *Songs of Salvation,* F.E.L.
"Care Is All It Takes," Jack Miffleton, *Even a Worm,* W.L.P.

Filmstrips

The Sacrifice of Abraham, #2, *Abraham, Father of Believers,* Roa
    Films
The Fir Tree, The Pumpkin, from *Holydays and Holidays,* Twenty-
    Third Publications
The Man for Others, Thomas Klise

Literature

Silverstein, Shel. *The Giving Tree.* New York: Harper and Row, 1964
Yamaguchi, Tohr. *Two Crabs and the Moonlight.* New York: Holt,
    Rinehart and Winston, 1965
Paulus, Trina. *Hope for the Flowers.* New York: Paulist Press, 1972

Preparation

1. Select a picture to illustrate what it means to sacrifice.

2. Write a short poem on what it means to sacrifice. Share the
poem during the celebration and any experience you can recall when
you had to sacrifice something in order for something else to occur.

54

Readings

1. John 3:16-19. Christ died for us, to teach us how to love.
2. Matthew 20:20-28. Imitate Jesus who came to serve.
3. Other: Mark 10:17-21

Homily Hints

Listen to the poems and the personal experiences. To sacrifice is to have a goal, a higher goal and to do what is necessary to achieve what is desired. In sports it means training, for a career it means study, for growth it means to make mistakes. All choices require some kind of sacrifice and all choices tell us something about ourselves and what we value. Share the various pictures illustrating the word "sacrifice." Do any commonalities exist in the paintings? Are all sacrifices necessarily sad or difficult? What role do our motives play in our choice of sacrifices? Can motives make some sacrifices pleasant? What was Jesus' sacrifice?

Prayer Experience

Jesus chose to sacrifice himself for people, for us. Prepare an opaque projector presentation using pictures of many, many people. Play and listen to a recording of "People" while pictures pass on the screen. Think about what you want to do with your life.

Gifts

Bread and wine, diploma, marriage license, poems, pictures.

Follow-up

Think about your own life and the many good things you have that make it happy. Are there some things, good things, you might share with someone else? Share one.

8

Forgiveness

Resources

Songs

"Pardon Your People," Carey Landry, *The Spirit Is A-Movin,* N.A.L.R.
"O Lord Have Mercy on Me," Lou Fortunate, William H. Sadlier, Inc.
"But Then Comes the Morning," Jack Miffleton, W.L.P.

Filmstrips

The Red Racer, The Dropout, Parables, Twenty-Third Publications
The Fight, #17, *Kree Finds the Way,* Roa Films
Penance: Sacrament of Reconciliation, Thomas Klise
Joseph, CEBCO/Standard Publishing
Forgiveness, #5, *Children of the Light,* Roa Films

Literature

Estes, Eleanor. *The Hundred Dresses.* New York: Harcourt, Brace,
     Jovanovich, 1944
Weimer, Rudolph Otto. *The Prodigal Son.* Minneapolis: Augsburg, 1967
Kay, Helen. *A Stocking for a Kitten.* Minneapolis: Augsburg, 1970
.... *Zaccheus.* Minneapolis: Augsburg, 1970

Preparation

1. Before the celebration ask the children to think about a time when they had done something wrong and had been forgiven. Perhaps it was at home, maybe in school or at the supermarket. Recall how they felt, what they thought, what they did.

2. Read Luke 15:11-32, the story of the Prodigal Son. Prepare a group to dramatize the reading—assign roles, teach dialogue, etc.

Ask non-actors to analyze the various characters and place themselves in the shoes of the character they identify with most. Suggest that they think about feelings, attitudes, past histories of their chosen character. What do they do in the story and why? What value seems most important?

Readings

1. Isaiah 44:21-23. The Lord rescues us from sin.
2. Luke 15:11-32. The Father loves us and forgives us.

Homily Hints

Listen to the children's recollections and comment accordingly. Announce the dramatization, explain the setting, bring on the actors. Allow everyone a chance to identify with his favorite character. Analyze the story with the children, listen to their ideas and insights. Tell them of the father's love for the son and our Heavenly Father's love for us and his wish for our happiness and growth. Forgiveness always helps us to grow.

Prayer Experience

On a slip of paper ask children to write a petition for forgiveness. Example: "For the times I was purposely mean, Lord, I ask forgiveness." Fold the paper, collect them, burn them in view of all. The celebrant can compose an appropriate prayer.

Gifts

Bread and wine, the ashes, the props from the dramatization.

Follow-up

Make a poster using a phrase from one of the readings or one that really says something to you. Hang it in your room as a reminder of your need to forgive and be forgiven.

9
Loyalty

Resources

Songs

"How Good Is the Lord," Carey Landry, N.A.L.R.
"If You Love Me Keep My Word," Lou Fortunate, William H. Sadlier,
    Inc.

Filmstrips

The Pumpkin Who Was Not a Squash, from *Holydays and Holidays,*
    Twenty-Third Publications
Hosea: Prophet of Love, #6, *Kings and Prophets,* Roa Films
Parables, Twenty-Third Publications

Literature

Pottebaum, Gerard. *99 Plus One.* Minneapolis: Augsburg, 1971

Preparation

1. Before the celebration have each child write a paragraph on a
person who was loyal to his country, or to a promise made, or to
another person, or to God. Suggest that they think about saints whose
lives they may have read or heard about or persons from history or
maybe even someone in contemporary times.

2. Cut out newspaper stories describing people who were loyal,
bring them to the celebration and be prepared to share your ideas
about what loyalty means to you.

Readings

1. 1 John 4:7-16. God loves us; we should love one another.
2. Matthew 22:34-40. The two great commands: love of God and of
   neighbor.
3. Other: Luke 10:25-37; Ephesians 3:14-21

Homily Hints

What persons have the children written about in their paragraphs? Ask them why each was loyal or what special reason caused them to act in the manner they did. Belief in a person who will act in a certain fashion is part of loyalty; so, too, is a promise made in good faith to act in a certain fashion. Ask children to write anonymous answers to this incomplete sentence on a piece of paper. The hardest part of being loyal is .... Collect the papers, read selected ones, make comments based on your own appreciation of the topic.

Prayer Experience

We are called to be loyal to the promises that were made for us at Baptism. Let the celebrant lead the community in a renewing of our baptismal promises. Pause between the different questions and ask everyone to think about the meaning of his assent to the promises.

Gifts

Bread, wine, paragraphs, written-on papers, newspaper stories.

Follow-up

Reflect on the many answers to the hardest part of being loyal. Choose one or two for yourself and try to develop positive habits of loyalty in your own life.

10

Cooperation

Resources

Songs

"Alive in Christ," Lou Fortunate, William H. Sadlier, Inc.
"I Must Remember," Lou Fortunate, William H. Sadlier, Inc.

Filmstrips

Exploring the Village, #11, Kree Finds the Way, Roa Films
Billy Beaver, from Holydays and Holidays, Twenty-Third Publications
Think of Others First, Guidance Associates

Literature

Anderson, Lonzo and Adams, Adrienne, Two Hundred Rabbits. New York: Viking Press, 1968
Ballard, Martin. The Emir's Son. New York: World Publishing Co., 1967

Preparation

1. Before the celebration ask each child to draw a series of six pictures depicting cooperation at home, at school, on the playground, in the store, on vacation, and at any one time they can think of. Bring pictures to the celebration.

2. Review the newspapers for one week before the celebration, looking for items where cooperation meant the difference between success and failure. Bring stories to the celebration.

Readings

1. 1 Thessalonians 5:14-18. Advice for the community.
2. John 6:1-13. The contribution of one helps all.

Homily Hints

Count with the children the variety of ways in which cooperation takes place at home, in school, etc., and listen to the retelling of the news stories highlighting cooperation. To cooperate doesn't always guarantee that everything will go the way you think it should go, but it is safe to say that more people will be satisfied at least partially if cooperation is sought. Everyone can write down and complete this sentence: "One thing I learned about cooperation today is ...." Call for response and make appropriate comments and suggestions.

Prayer Experience

Pray together the Prayer of St. Francis.

Gifts

Bread, wine, artwork, news stories, learning statements.

Follow-up

Read over the Prayer of St. Francis; try to memorize the whole prayer, or at least a favored phrase. Pray with Francis from time to time and apply the prayer to your life. A good biography of the renowned Christian would be worth reading.

11

Honesty

Resources

Songs

"If You Love Me Keep My Word," Lou Fortunate, William H. Sadlier, Inc.

"Love One Another," Germaine Habjan, *Songs of Salvation,* F.E.L.

Filmstrips

Somebody's Cheating, Guidance Associates
The Candidate, Parables, Twenty-Third Publications
The Trouble With Truth, First Things, Guidance Associates
Exploring Moral Values, Warren Schloat Productions

Literature

Ness, Evaline. *Sam, Bangs, and Moonshine.* New York: Holt, Rinehart and Winston, 1966

Preparation

1. Make individual colorful banners on the theme of honesty and bring them to the celebration for decoration.

2. Before the celebration divide the group into sets of two, distribute dittoed copies of quotations about honesty, perhaps taken from *Bartlett's Book of Familiar Quotations.* Let each couple discuss a chosen quotation in terms of the following points: "One thing I disagree with about what the quotation says is ...." "One thing I agree with about the quotation is ...." "The quotation confused me when it said ...." Celebrants can use other incomplete sentences to expand the dialogue.

Readings

1. Romans 15:2-3, 5-7. Honesty is a way of loving others.
2. Mark 4:3-9, 14-20. Honesty means being open to God's word.

Homily Hints

Suggest that children carry their banners in a procession (parade) around the place of celebration. Sing an accompanying song. Everyone will be able to see them. When the procession is over and the banners hung in place, ask the banner-makers to let you in on some of the things that were discussed while the banners were being created. Make comments. Take time to listen to the various quotations and responses to the questions. Questions such as "Is honesty always the best policy?" will be raised along with many comments about recent political events. The story of Pinocchio and his nose that grew every time he told a lie could be used to make many points on honesty in simple terms.

Prayer Experience

Pray together a contemporary version of Psalm 119:1-8.

Gifts

Bread, wine, banners, quotations and responses.

Follow-up

Memorize one of the quotations brought out in the homily. Create your own banner or poster illustrating what it means and hang it somewhere as a reminder to you to always strive toward being an honest person.

12
Care and Concern

Resources

Songs

"You Are the Way," Joe Wise, *Watch With Me,* N.A.L.R.
"Go Forth," James Haas, *Rainbow Songs,* Morehouse-Barlow
"God Has Visited His People," James Haas, *Rainbow Songs,* More-house-Barlow
"Care Is All It Takes," Jack Miffleton, *Even a Worm,* W.L.P.

Filmstrips

Amos: Prophet of Judgment, #5, *Kings and Prophets,* Roa Films
The Rescue, Parables, Twenty-Third Publications
The Missionary, #16, *Kree Finds the Way,* Roa Films
At Work Within the Church, Lutheran Church Press

Literature

Ness, Evaline. *Do You Have the Time, Lydia?* New York: E. P. Dutton and Co., 1974
Sommerfelt, Aimee. *The Road to Agra.* New York: Criterion, 1961

Preparation

1. Divide the class into groups and let each group make a mobile depicting as many instances of man showing care and concern for his fellowman.

2. Divide class into groups and let them choose some voluntary action that will express their care and concern for younger kids, older folks, the community, the Church, etc. Suggest that they be prepared to talk about their experience.

Readings

1. 1 Peter 4:8-11. Use gifts in service.
2. John 13:34-35. Love as sign of disciples.
3. Other: Romans 13:7-10; Luke 14:12-14; Luke 17:3-6

Homily Hints

Let the groups explain their mobiles and the thoughts they had while creating them. Listen to the other groups explain their voluntary actions, good deeds, etc. Make appropriate comments.

Prayer Experience

In creating a prayer of the faithful ask celebrators to complete this sentence in their own words: "One thing I learned about care and concern for others is .... and I thank you, Lord." Everyone can repeat "Thank you, Lord."

Gifts

Bread, wine, mobiles, list of care and concern.

Follow-up

For an established time following the celebration the group can save money (sacrifice again) in a "We Care" can. The money can be assigned to a worthy cause.

13
Suffering

Resources

Songs

"Even Then," Huub Oosterhuis, N.A.L.R.
"Prayer for the Sick," Lou Fortunate, William H. Sadlier, Inc.
"The Love of God," Lou Fortunate, William H. Sadlier, Inc.

Filmstrips

Learning and Growing, #14, *Kree Finds the Way,* Roa Films
The Fir Tree, The Pumpkin, from *Holydays and Holidays,* Twenty-
    Third Publications
My Name Is Jesus, Roa Films

Literature

Sachs, Marilyn. *The Bear's House.* New York: Doubleday, 1971

Preparation

1. Think about a person you know who is suffering in any way whatsoever and go out of your way to relieve that pain.

2. Go to the stories in the bible that have Jesus relieving the sufferings of man. How many kinds of handicaps did he remove from those who asked him? The blind, the deaf, the lame, the dumb, the paralyzed and the pained came to Jesus seeking cures and he cured them. Compare these stories with contemporary events and come to the celebration prepared for discussion.

Readings

1. Matthew 8:1-17. Jesus spends a day helping the suffering
2. James 5:14-16. The Church community helps those who suffer

Homily Hints

Ask children to talk about the various kinds of suffering they thought about and what they did to relieve the different situations. Comment that pain doesn't need to be great to merit our attention. Sometimes a kind word or a smile does a great deal to make things better. Share ideas how people today need healing, not miraculously as with Jesus, but in whatever human ways possible. People blind to new ideas need to be made relatively comfortable in a world of change and people who never hear the cries of those in need must be encouraged by our words and actions to listen and respond.

Prayer Experience

Listen to a modern song like "Try a Little Kindness," sing along or listen and reflect on the words.

Gifts

Bread, wine, a cane, hearing aid, crutches.

Follow-up

Make your own collage composed of signs of suffering and keep it handy. Pause each night before sleep to think about the sufferings you may have caused but also those you may have helped to relieve.

14
Using Talents

Resources

Songs

"All That I Am," Sebastian Temple, *Sing, People of God, Sing,* Franciscan Communications Center
"Of My Hands," Ray Repp, *Mass For Young Americans,* F.E.L.
"Everybody's Got to Grow," Jack Miffleton, *Even A Worm,* W.L.P.

Filmstrips

Images of the New Man Series, Thomas Klise
Man for Others, Thomas Klise
Festival of Art, William H. Sadlier, Inc.

Literature

Lionni, Leo. *Frederick.* New York: Pantheon, 1967

Preparation

1. Before the celebration ask the children to think about, then write down at least two talents each has. Then encourage them to discover a magazine picture that would illustrate those talents.

2. Read Matthew 25:14-30, the Parable of the Talents. Prepare groups to dramatize the readings, assigning roles, teaching dialogue, etc. Ask non-acting participants to analyze the various characters and place themselves in the shoes of the character they identify with most. Suggest they think about feelings, attitudes, past experiences of their chosen characters. What value do they cherish and who might they represent?

Readings

1. 1 Corinthians 12:4-13. All gifts are to be used for unity of the Church.
2. Matthew 25:14-30. Parable of the talents.
3. Other: Romans 12:3-13; Luke 19:11-26; Ephesians 1:3-14.

Homily Hints

Listen to and affirm all the talents that are present in this place of celebration. To perfect all these talents would be to sing a hymn of praise to God. Announce the play, set the scene, bring on the actors and actresses. Encourage everyone, teachers too, to identify with a favored character. Following the play, analyze the play, the characters, the lessons taught. God wants us to grow, to use the gifts he gives us freely to bring about a better world.

Prayer Experience

Sing the song, *"All That I Am,"* and add gestures to accompany the lyrics.

Gifts

Bread, wine, talent sheets, props from the play.

Follow-up

Write a "Thank You" note to your parents for helping you develop the talents you've been given and pledge to continue developing these gifts from God.

15
Hope

Resources

Songs

I Believe in the Sun, Carey Landry, *Hi God!* N.A.L.R.
Spirit of God, James Haas, *Rainbow Songs,* Morehouse-Barlow

Filmstrips

Joseph, Pflaum Standard
The Fir Tree, from *Holydays and Holidays,* Twenty-Third Publications
Ezekiel: Prophet of Hope, #10, *Kings and Prophets,* Roa Films

Literature

Kraus, Robert. *Leo the Late Bloomer.* New York: Windmill Books
and E. P. Dutton, 1971

Preparation

1. Before the celebration list five ways we can help people to hope
when things look bleak. What signs of hope can we share with
whom?

2. Signs of hope abound like the Red Cross, the Cancer Crusade
symbol, the Dove or Peace symbol and many others. Brainstorm before the celebration as many signs of hope in our world as you can.
A good idea might be to think of the many ways men suffer and the
signs of hope held out to them. What contemporary men and women
are signs of hope. Bring copies of the symbols of hope and pictures
of the people to the celebration.

Readings

1. Hebrews 4:14-16. Jesus shares our weaknesses.
2. Luke 22:39-46. Jesus is afraid and turns to his Father.

Homily Hints

Hear the many ways in which men can add to the store of human kindness and see the many signs of hope that exist in a world that for many seems hopeless. The quest for peace begins with the individual's efforts to bring it about in his own life, in his own situation. The men and women named as signs of hope have goals and need support. Brainstorm ways to continue to bring hope to our world. Jesus is the great sign of hope. If we take his commands to heart, hope has to enter the lives of those around us.

Prayer Experience

Divide the group in two and pray antiphonally Psalm 62.

Gifts

Bread, wine, lists, symbols of hope, pictures of men and women.

Follow-up

Pledge a certain amount of money, time or your talent to a cause, a person or an idea that needs you, then make a contract with yourself to do what you decide.

16

Temptation

Resources

Songs

"Growing," James Haas, *Rainbow Songs,* Morehouse-Barlow
"I Must Remember," Lou Fortunate, William H. Sadlier, Inc.

Filmstrips

Baptism and Temptation of Jesus, #6, *Good News of Christ,* Roa
    Films
Charles Caterpillar, from *Holydays and Holidays,* Twenty-Third Pub-
    lications

Literature

Matsuno, Masako. *Taro and the Tofu.* World Publishing Co., 1962

Preparation

1. Before the celebration watch the filmstrip, *Charles Caterpillar.* Let
the children write these sentences and their own answers about the
filmstrip. "One thing I liked about the story —————." "One
thing I didn't like about the story —————." "One thing that confused me in the story —————." "One thing I learned from the
story —————."

2. Write a story describing how a person deals with a situation in
his or her life where a choice must be made between doing something known to be right and good, and doing something wrong. Write
two endings to your story, and justify both endings.

Readings

1. James 1:2-5. Testing is a time for growing.
2. Matthew 4:1-15. Jesus' experience of temptation.

Homily Hints

Ask the children to relate the filmstrip story and the points they enjoyed, didn't like, were confused by and learned. (A handy teacher's guide accompanies the strip.) No matter the temptation or the outcome, man is responsible for whatever action he decides to take. God has given us the freedom of choice, but not all decisions, moral or otherwise, are always easy to make. Listen to some of the other stories that were composed and reasons behind the different endings. What gospel stories relate to temptation and what light does Jesus shed on this human experience?

Prayer Experience

Reflect quietly on a moment in your life when you were faced with a major decision. Speak quietly your own prayer for courage to continue making decisions that will help you grow.

Gifts

Bread, wine, children's written responses and stories.

Follow-up

Parents, relatives, teachers and many others continually help us to make decisions that are good for our growth. Write a letter to someone whose life is an inspiration to you, thanking him or her for giving you something valuable to think about and cherish.

17

Redemption

Resources

Songs

"I Must Remember," Lou Fortunate, William H. Sadlier, Inc.
"But Then Comes the Morning," Jack Miffleton, W.L.P.
"From the Voices of Children," Neil Blunt, *No Time Like the Present,*
   W.L.P.

Literature

Lionni, Leo. *The Greentail Mouse.* New York: Pantheon, 1973

Preparation

1. Before the celebration have the children create individual two-sided collages depicting sin and evil in the world on one side and signs of redemption on the other.

2. Read to the group the story of the woman who was a sinner, Luke 7: 36-50, the parable of the unforgiving servant, Matthew 18: 23-35, and the greatest commandment of them all, Matthew 22: 34-40. Have the children write updated versions of the passages, or a short essay on what Jesus is telling us about sin, mercy and forgiveness.

Readings

1. Ephesians 4:31-5:2. Give up sin, and love as Jesus did.
2. Luke 5:1-11. Jesus calls sinners to follow him.

Homily Hints

Ask for explanations of two-sided collages. How do the children interpret evil and redemption? Listen to the updated versions of scripture and comment on the essays. Sin is personal; it is also communal. We sin by our actions but we also sin through our lack of action. Sin is "out there," but it is also very much a part of us. But Jesus tells us we are saved, we are loved by God who wants us to share that love in as many ways as we can.

Prayer Experience

Jesus invariably told the sinner to "go and sin no more" and his wish for mankind is peace. Let the children share with one another a genuine sign of forgiveness, a handshake, perhaps, and say from deep within a personal wish for peace.

Gifts

Bread, wine, collages, updated scripture versions.

Follow-up

Compose your personal prayer of sorrow for the times you were willfully hurtful or mean. Reflect on what you can do to make up for the wrong you did or permitted, then try to do it.

18
Joy

Resources

Songs

"Go Now in Peace," Joe Wise, *Watch With Me,* N.A.L.R.
"Happy Is the Man," Dan Schutte, S.J., *Neither Silver Nor Gold,*
    N.A.L.R.
"Sing for Joy," James Haas, *Rainbow Songs,* Morehouse-Barlow
"To Be Alive," Ray Repp, *Hymnal for Young Christians,* Vol. II, F.E.L.
"I've Got That Joy, Joy, Joy," Traditional

Filmstrips

Journey to Joy Series, Concordia Films
A Time for Singing, Concordia Films

Preparation

1. Select and listen to a few happy upbeat songs expressive of joy.
"I've Got That Joy, Joy, Joy, Down in My Heart" comes to mind
immediately, along with "Sing for Joy." Ask children to create gestures to accompany the songs, learn them and the songs well and
come to the celebration.

2. Ask each child to interview family members, friends, and relatives, asking them for their definitions of "joy." Secondly ask them
if they would be willing to talk about an experience of great joy in
their lives. It would be good for the interviewers to write down the
definitions and recall the highlight of the various experiences.

Readings

1. Philippians 1:2-11. Paul's joy in the faith of Philippians.
2. Luke 1:39-55. Mary expresses her joy in God's love.

Homily Hints

The theme is joy, so everyone can listen to or sing along with the joyful songs, watching or joining in the gestures the children have chosen. Reflect on the feelings everyone will have and ask for their ideas on joy. Talk with the interviewers, listen to the definitions and the joyful experiences. Is there a qualitative difference between a joy-filled experience and a happy time? Are there any common threads running through the definitions and events? What are they? The life of a follower of Jesus is a joy-filled life, not that all experiences are happy, because Jesus lived, died, and rose to new life.

Prayer Experience

In a communal prayer let the children offer examples of joyful times and events in their lives whereupon the group can respond with a prayerful "Thank you, Lord."

Gifts

Bread, wine, dancing shoes, definitions.

Follow-up

Look up and select a quotation on "joy" in *Bartlett's Book of Familiar Quotations,* find a photograph that illustrates the quotation, then join the two in holy card fashion. Give your creation away as a simple gift.

19

Covenant

Resources

Songs

"What a Great Thing It Is," Ray Repp, *Allelu,* F.E.L.
"Love One Another," Germaine Habjan, *Songs of Salvation,* F.E.L.

Filmstrips

The Covenant, #4, *Moses and the Covenant,* Roa Films
Cup and Covenant, Thomas Klise

Literature

Perrine, Mary. *Salt Boy. Boston:* Houghton Mifflin, 1968

Preparation

1. A covenant is a contract. Before the celebration discuss many different kinds of contracts/promises man can make and think of ways to depict them. A handshake can be a contract, as can a kiss. A marriage license is a contract, as is a pledge made to another. Let the group create a collage/montage of all the contracts they know and can illustrate.

2. Before the celebration invite a lawyer from the community to speak to the group about contracts. Questions can be prepared beforehand about who can make contracts, what constitutes legality and what happens when a contract is broken. Come to the celebration prepared to discuss what the guest spoke about.

Readings

1. Exodus 19:3-6. God makes a covenant with his people.
2. John 14:15-21. Jesus speaks of the *new* covenant.
3. Other: Matthew 5:14-19

Homily Hints

Decorate the place of celebration with the collage/montage. Discuss the many types of contracts the children became aware of and chose to illustrate. Refer to the guest speaker's comments and apply some of the selected questions to different contracts in the art form. Covenants were made and broken between God and the people of Israel in the Old Testament. When the covenants were broken, it was always the people, but God continues to offer mankind the gift of his love. He sent Jesus who was himself rejected and yet God continues to want to draw people to himself. That's an offer you don't want to refuse!

Prayer Experience

Think about your closest friend and the wordless contract between the two of you. Think how much you like being together, working and playing. It is the same gift of friendship God offers us, and it is ours for the taking.

Gifts

Bread, wine, collage/montage, notes from guest's lecture.

Follow-up

Make a contract with yourself for a limited action and a specified time. Keep to it and reflect upon the values of what you contracted to do.

20
Prophets

Resources

Songs

"Till All My People Are One," Ray Repp, *Come Alive,* F.E.L.
"Friend of the Prophet," Neil Blunt, *Possible Gospel,* N.A.L.R.

Filmstrips

Abraham, Father of Believers, Roa Films
Jonah, Joseph, CEBCO/Standard Publishing

Preparation

1. Before the celebration help the children select articles from newspapers about persons who are calling for reforms or changes in society. Write a brief playlet about one of the articles and perform it during the celebration.

2. Before the celebration have a discussion on prophets, the religious ones, social ones, political ones. Determine the qualities necessary for becoming a prophet and the possible rewards open to someone pursuing the prophet's life. Then ask each child to write a want-ad for the classified section of the newspaper, looking for someone to be a prophet. Bring the ads to the celebration.

Readings

1. Jeremiah 1:4-10, 17-19. God calls Jeremiah to be a prophet.
2. Luke 4:16-30. Jesus appears as a prophet to his neighbors.
3. Other: Isaiah 6:1-10

Homily Hints

The children in preparing the playlet will have talked about what a prophet is and does. Before the dramatization discuss the story they'll do and why it is prophetic. Ask them if they would like to be a prophet and why. Bring on the players, enjoy the action, and when complete discuss what took place. Call for a recitation of the "want-ads." How are prophets usually received and what happens to them frequently? Are prophets generally enthusiastic about functioning in that role? Why? Why not?

Prayer Experience

The celebrant can tell briefly the stories of some Old and New Testament prophets and what they were calling for, then mention some contemporary persons whose lives seem to be prophetic. Let each child pray quietly for the courage to stand up for the truth and justice in his own world, in his own way.

Gifts

Bread, wine, want-ads, props from play.

Follow-up

Read a biography of a contemporary prophet in any field. Select one of his or her quotes, make it your own and try to live out the particular value.

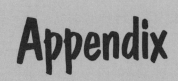
Appendix

Selected Resources

MULTI-MEDIA PROGRAMS

Alpha Corporation of America
1421 Armour Boulevard
Mundelein, IL 60060

Cathedral Films
2921 West Alameda Avenue
Burbank, CA 91505

CEBCO/Standard Publishing
(formerly Pflaum Standard)
2285 Arbor Blvd.
Dayton, OH 45439

Concordia Publishing House
3558 S. Jefferson Avenue
St. Louis, MO 63118

Don Bosco Filmstrips
Box T
New Rochelle, NY 10802

Family Filmstrips
5823 Santa Monica Boulevard
Hollywood, CA 90038

Guidance Associates
23 Washington Avenue
Pleasantville, NY 10570

Thomas Klise Co. Inc.
P.O. Box 3418
Peoria, IL 61414

Lutheran Church Press
2900 Queen Lane
Philadelphia, PA 19129

Our Sunday Visitor
Catechetical Guild Department
Noll Plaza
Huntington, IN 46750

Roa Films
1696 North Astor Street
Milwaukee, WI 53202

William H. Sadlier, Inc.
11 Park Place
New York, NY 10007

Warren Schloat Productions
Tompkins Avenue
Pleasantville, NY 10570

Teleketics
Franciscan Communications
1229 South Santee Street
Los Angeles, CA 90015

Twenty-Third Publications
P.O. Box 180
West Mystic, CT 06388

MUSIC AND RECORDS

Joe Wise

A New Day (W.L.P.), Welcome In (N.A.L.R.), Gonna Sing My Lord (W.L.P.), Hand in Hand (W.L.P.), Watch With Me (N.A.L.R.), Close Your Eyes, I've Got a Surprise (N.A.L.R.).

Ray Repp

Mass for Young Americans (F.E.L.), The Time Has Not Come True (F.E.L.), Allelu (F.E.L.), Sing Praise! Sing Praise to God! (F.E.L.), Come Alive (F.E.L.).

Jack Miffleton

With Skins and Steel (W.L.P.), Come Out! (W.L.P.), Even a Worm (W.L.P.), Alle, Alle (W.L.P.), No Time Like the Present (W.L.P.), Some Young Carpenter (W.L.P.).

Carey Landry

Hi God! (N.A.L.R.), The Spirit Is A'Movin (N.A.L.R.), Yes Lord (N.A.L.R.), Great Things Happen (N.A.L.R.).

Robert Blue

Run Come See (F.E.L.).

W. F. Jabusch

Whatsoever You Do (Acta Foundation).

James E. Haas

Rainbow Songs (Morehouse-Barlow).

Sebastian Temple

Sing, People of God, Sing (Franciscan Communications Center).

The Dameans

Songs of the New Creation (F.E.L.), Tell the World (F.E.L.).

Medical Mission Sisters

Joy Is Like the Rain (Vanguard), Knock, Knock (Vanguard).

Acta Foundation
4848 N. Clark Street
Chicago, IL 60640

F.E.L. Publications
1925 Pontius Avenue
Los Angeles, CA 90025

Franciscan Communications Center
1229 S. Santee Street
Los Angeles, CA 90015

North American Liturgy Resources
300 E. McMillan Street
Cincinnati, OH 45219

Morehouse-Barlow Co.
14 East 41st Street
New York, NY 10017

Vanguard Music Corp.
250 West 47th Street
New York, NY 10019

World Library Publications
2145 Central Parkway
Cincinnati, OH 45214

PERIODICALS

The following periodicals publish background material that will prove useful to persons involved in planning liturgies with young Christians.

Liturgy Magazine
>   Every issue of this publication from the Liturgical Conference is worth looking into; occasional special issues deal specifically with liturgy for children. Liturgical Conference, 1330 Massachusetts Avenue, N.W., Washington, D.C. 20005.

Folk Mass and Modern Liturgy
>   A relatively new resource to assist all who are engaged in planning or leading worship. Resource Publications, 6244 Rainbow Drive, San Jose, CA 95129.

Newsletter of Bishops' Committee on the Liturgy
>   Bishops' Committee on the Liturgy, 1312 Massachusetts Avenue, N.W., Washington, D.C. 20005.

A.I.M. (Aids In Ministry)
>   Paluch Publications, Box 367, Princeton Junction, NJ 08550

From the following magazines, selected articles are indicated; these articles will be of direct interest to those who work with children in worship.

Catechist
>   2285 Arbor Boulevard, Dayton, OH 45439.

Issue	Article
March, 1968	(Entire issue on the subject of celebration)
January, 1969	Teen Celebration on Brotherhood
October, 1969	Prayers Children Pray
January, 1970	The Kingdom of Heaven Is Like a Lollipop
March, 1972	A Children's Mass for Pentecost
	Toward a Creative Liturgical Experience
September, 1972	Liturgy: Then and Now
January, 1973	Dramatization
April, 1973	The New Rite of Confirmation
September, 1973	Rhythms of Celebration
October, 1973	Liturgy and Learning
February, 1974	A Primer on Liturgy

March, 1974   Planning Liturgy
April, 1974   Liturgy and Catechetics
September, 1974   Guidelines for Children's Masses
October, 1974   When Are Children Ready for Confession?
March, 1975   Brooklyn's 9 O'clock Mass

Religion Teacher's Journal
     Twenty-Third Publications, P. O. Box 180, West Mystic, CT 06388.

Issue	*Article*
January, 1969	Make Your Own Liturgies
February, 1969	Liturgy Room for Grade-Schoolers
April, 1969	Celebration in Christ
May/June, 1969	Children's Mass
September, 1969	Toward a Sacred Dance
November, 1969	Psalms for Youngsters
	Scripture Celebration on Space Exploration
January, 1970	We Celebrate Together
February, 1970	A Christmas Seder
May, 1970	A Catechetical Liturgy Room
October, 1970	Praise the Lord With Banners
January, 1971	A Celebration for Small Children
April, 1971	Religious Celebration Workshop
May/June, 1971	A Pentecost Celebration
September, 1971	Whose Language: What Gets Communicated?
March, 1972	JAPAM: Teaching Prayer Today
	Walk In Beauty: An Indian Liturgy
April, 1972	A Rainbow Walk
October, 1972	Classroom Liturgies
Nov/Dec, 1972	Advent Wreath Ceremony for Middle-Schoolers
February, 1973	A Lesson for Lent
	A Plan for Penance
April, 1973	Celebration in the Teacher/Learner Process
	The First Class After Easter
September, 1973	God Language: Limits and Possibilities
	Celebrating Baptism
Nov/Dec, 1973	A Catechetical Mass
	Exploring God's Book
January, 1974	Confirmation: Junior High Style
	Com-union

February, 1974	Religious Drama
	Celebrating Love
	Easter Sunday Liturgy
March, 1974	Cartoons Can Help You Teach
	Role Playing
April, 1974	Finding the Bible
	Slides for Confirmation
May/June, 1974	Teacher Commissioning Ceremony
September, 1974	Pilgrimages for Pilgrims
	Celebrating Myself
October, 1974	Celebrating Thanksgiving
	Symbols and Senses
	Thanksgiving, Tabernacles and Eucharist
	Some Basics for Using Scripture
Nov/Dec, 1974	Things to Do for Advent
	Classes on Prayer
	Hearing the Word in Song
February, 1975	Slump Celebrations
	Things to Do for Lent
March, 1975	Developing Children's Liturgies
April, 1975	Let's Take a Tree
	Perceptive Film Probing
May/June, 1975	Parables for Primaries
	Sacraments: Signs of Human Development

Today's Parish

Twenty-Third Publications, P. O. Box 180, West Mystic, CT 06388

Issue	*Article*
April, 1973	Mother's Day Liturgy
Sept/Oct, 1973	Little People's Liturgies
Jan/Feb, 1974	Create A Climate of Prayer for Lent
	Rite On
March/April, 1974	Creating Meaningful Liturgical Experiences
May/June, 1974	Father's Day Liturgy
September, 1974	Ways to Build Christian Community
January, 1975	Team Building the Liturgy
February, 1975	Why Can't I Pray at Mass?
March, 1975	Celebrating Anointing
	Holy Week Programs
April, 1975	Mother's Day Liturgy
May/June, 1975	Youth Pentecost Liturgy
	Ritual Opening of Church Doors

BOOKS

Bucher, Sister Janet. *Run With Him*. North American Liturgy Resources, 300 E. McMillan Street, Cincinnati, OH 45219

Caprio, Betsy. *Experiments in Prayer*. Ave Maria Press, Notre Dame, IN 46556

Directory for Masses With Children. U.S.C.C. Publications, 1312 Massachusetts Avenue, N.W., Washington, D.C. 20005

Faucher, Rev. Thomas, and Neiland, Ione. *Touching God*. Ave Maria Press, Notre Dame, IN 46556

Haas, James E. *Shout Hooray*. Morehouse-Barlow Co., 14 E. 41st Street, New York, NY 10017

————. *Make A Joyful Noise*. Morehouse-Barlow Co.

————. *Praise the Lord*. Morehouse-Barlow Co.

Jamison, Andrew, O.F.M. *Liturgies for Children*. St. Anthony Messenger Press, 1615 Republic Street, Cincinnati, OH 45210

Landry, Rev. Carey, and Kinghorn, Carol Jean. *Hi God!* North American Liturgy Resources, 300 E. McMillan Street, Cincinnati, OH 45219

LeBlanc, Etienne, and Talbott, Sister Mary Rose. *How Green Is Green?* Ave Maria Press, Notre Dame, IN 46556

Miffleton, Jack. *Come Out*. World Library Publications, 2145 Central Parkway, Cincinnati, OH 45214

————. *Even a Worm*. World Library Publications.

Rabalais, Sister Maria, and Hall, Rev. Howard. *Children Celebrate*. Paulist Press, 1865 Broadway, New York, NY 10023

————, Hall, Rev. Howard, and Vavasseur, Rev. Donald. *Come! Be Reconciled*. Paulist Press, 1865 Broadway, New York, NY 10023

Sloyan, Virginia, and Huck, Gabe. *Children's Liturgies*. Liturgical Conference, 1330 Massachusetts Avenue, N.W., Washington, D.C. 20005

————. *Signs, Songs and Stories*. Liturgical Conference, 1330 Massachusetts Avenue, N.W., Washington, D.C. 20005

Tietjen, Mary Louise. *Alleluia Days*. Twenty-Third Publications, P. O. Box 180, West Mystic, CT 06388